Awesome Animal
Science Projects

ANN BENBOW AND COLIN MABLY

ILLUSTRATIONS BY TOM LABAFF

Enslow Elementary
an imprint of
Enslow Publishers, Inc.
40 Industrial Road
Box 398
Berkeley Heights, NJ 07922
USA

http://www.enslow.com

Enslow Elementary, an imprint of Enslow Publishers, Inc.

Enslow Elementary® is a registered trademark of Enslow Publishers, Inc.

Library of Congress Cataloging-in-Publication Data

Benbow, Ann.
    Awesome animal science projects / Ann Benbow and Colin Mably.
      p. cm. — (Real life science experiments)
    Includes bibliographical references and index.
    Summary: "Presents several easy-to-do science experiments about animals and animal behavior"—
Provided by publisher.
    ISBN-13: 978-0-7660-3148-7
    ISBN-10: 0-7660-3148-9
    1. Animals—Experiments—Juvenile literature. 2. Animal behavior—Experiments—Juvenile literature.
3. Zoology projects—Juvenile literature. I. Mably, Colin. II. Title.
    QL52.6.B46 2010
    590.78—dc22
                                     2008023932

Printed in the United States of America

10 9 8 7 6 5 4 3 2 1

To Our Readers: We have done our best to make sure all Internet Addresses in this book were active and appropriate when we went to press. However, the authors and the publisher have no control over and assume no liability for the material available on those Internet sites or on other Web sites they may link to. Any comments or suggestions can be sent by e-mail to comments@enslow.com or to the address on the back cover.

♻ Enslow Publishers, Inc., is committed to printing our books on recycled paper. The paper in every book contains 10% to 30% post-consumer waste (PCW). The cover board on the outside of each book contains 100% PCW. Our goal is to do our part to help young people and the environment too!

Illustration Credits: Tom LaBaff

Photo Credits: bbbsheep, p. 12; David Tipling/NHPA/Photoshot, p. 36; Dean Pomerleau, p. 44; © Sara Robinson/iStockphoto.com, p. 32; Shutterstock, pp. 8, 16, 20, 24, 28, 40

Cover Photo: Shutterstock

Contents

Experiments with a 🎗 symbol feature **Ideas for Your Science Fair.**

Introduction

There are many different types of animals on Earth. You may know a lot of these, such as dogs, cats, birds, and fish. But there are many other kinds that may be new to you, such as jellyfish and giant squids!

Animals, no matter what their size, live in places where they can find food and safety. Many animals blend in with their surroundings so that it is hard to see them. Other animals, like polar bears, need to survive in cold conditions and have thick fur and lots of fat to keep them warm. Birds' beaks are shaped to help them grab different kinds of food.

You can use this book to learn many things about animals and their behavior. You will be asking questions about animals and doing experiments with them. You will make observations and find answers. By the end, you will know a lot more about animals than you do now. You will also know more about science!

Science Fair Ideas

The investigations in this book will help you learn how to do experiments. After every investigation, you will find ideas for science fair projects. You may want to try one of these ideas, or you might think of a better project.

This book has a Learn More section. The books and Web sites in this section can give you more ideas for science fair projects.

Remember, science is all about asking questions. A science fair gives you the chance to investigate your own questions and record your results. It also lets you share your findings with your fellow scientists.

Safety First!

These are important rules to follow as you experiment.

1 Always have an adult nearby when doing experiments.

2 Follow instructions with care, especially safety warnings.

3 Never experiment with electrical outlets.

4 Use safety scissors, and have an adult handle any sharp objects.

5 Use only alcohol thermometers, never mercury!

6 Stay in a safe place if making outdoor observations.

7 Treat living things with care. Some may sting or be poisonous!

8 Keep your work area clean and organized.

9 Clean up and put materials away when you are done.

10 Always wash your hands when you are finished.

What Seeds Do Different Birds Like?

Which birds like to eat which seeds? Write down your ideas and your reasons for them.

Now Let's Find Out!

1 Fill one bird feeder with sunflower seeds. Fill the other feeder with millet seeds.

2 **Ask an adult** to hang the bird feeders outside where you can see them. They should be the same height from the ground and very close together.

Things You Will Need

an adult
2 identical bird feeders
sunflower and millet seeds
place to hang the bird feeders
bird field guide
notebook and pen
binoculars (optional)

3 At the same time every day for two weeks, spend an hour observing the birds that visit each feeder. **Ask an adult** to help you identify the birds using the bird field guide.

4 What kinds of birds seem to like the sunflower seeds?
What birds seem to like the millet seeds? Do some birds
eat both kinds of seeds? Why do you think this is so?

What Seeds Do Different Birds Like?

An Explanation

Birds are adapted to eating different types of food. Small birds, such as sparrows and chickadees, like to eat small seeds, such as millet. These birds also usually eat their food off the ground. Larger birds, like blue jays and cardinals,

FACT: Birds help to spread seeds without meaning to. When a bird eats a berry, the seeds inside end up in the bird's waste. The bird may fly far before it deposits its waste. In this way, seeds are carried away from the plant that made the berry and the plant can grow in a new area.

A waxwing eats a berry.

can eat the larger sunflower seeds. Seed-eating birds usually have short, strong bills to crack the seeds.

 ## Ideas for Your Science Fair

- Are birds more likely to get seeds from a feeder or the ground?

- Are more birds attracted to a feeder in the winter or the summer?

- Which birds are attracted to pieces of fruit?

A chickadee's beak is just right for eating tiny millet seeds.

A cardinal's beak works for sunflower seeds.

Are Earthworms Attracted to Light?

Do earthworms, who live underground, seem attracted to light or not? Write down your ideas and your reasons for them.

Now Let's Find Out!

Things You Will Need

4 earthworms from your yard or a park

foil or plastic square pan (approx. 9 x 13 inches, or 23 x 33 cm)

moist, loose soil

darkened room

flashlight with strong beam

clock or watch

cup of water

notebook and pen

1 Fill the pan with the soil. Do this experiment in a dark room. Make sure you have just enough light to see what you are doing. Put two earthworms at one end of the pan and the other two earthworms at the other end.

2 Shine the flashlight onto one end of the pan and hold it very still. Observe what the two earthworms do for 10 minutes.

3 Write or draw your observations in your notebook. Make sure your earthworms do not dry out during your experiment. You can sprinkle them with a little water if they look dry.

4 Move your light to the other side of the pan. Now what do those earthworms do? Again, write or draw your observations.

Are Earthworms Attracted to Light?

An Explanation

An earthworm's body fits its burrowing lifestyle. It has a head at one end and a tail at the other. Its body is divided into a series of segments which help it to move.

Since they live underground, most earthworms are very sensitive to light and tend to move away from it. They do

FACT: The Kinabalu giant earthworm can grow up to 70 cm long (almost 28 in). It lives on the island of Borneo and is a shiny greenish blue color.

Kinabalu giant earthworm

not have eyes, but they do have tiny organs on their backs and head that sense light. Because it has no eyes, the earthworm cannot see its food. Instead, the worm's prostomium, just in front of its mouth, can tell the difference between food it likes and food it does not like.

 ## Ideas for Your Science Fair

- Do earthworms like dry or moist soil?
- What do earthworms do around other earthworms?
- Are earthworms sensitive to sound?

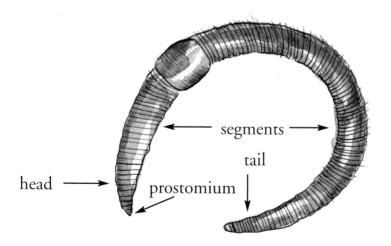

head ⟶   prostomium   segments   tail

How Do Ants Behave Around Their Home?

What kinds of things do ants do in and near their home? Write down your ideas and your reasons for them.

Now Let's Find Out!

1 In summer, find a place where black ants live close to your home. Ants usually live under very small mounds with a hole in the top. You will likely find one in a driveway, on a sidewalk, in your yard, or in a playground.

Things You Will Need

black ant home

magnifying glass (never look toward the sun through a magnifying glass)

notebook and pen

2 When you find an ant home, look at it closely. What does the ant home seem to be made from? Where do you think the material has come from?

3 Look at the ants moving around the ant home,

first with your eyes and then with the magnifying glass. What are different ants doing? Are they all doing the same thing? Do the ants stay in the same area, or do some go away and come back? Do they go inside their ant home?

4 Watch the ants for at least 15 minutes. Write or draw your observations about the ants.

5 Do you think that the ants live together in their ant home? How do the ants seem to be helping each other to survive?

How Do Ants Behave Around Their Home?

An Explanation

Common black ants make their homes in the ground. They dig tunnels and chambers. The material they remove is piled outside their home entrance. It is usually sandy material. Worker ants are the ones that dig out the spaces. They also go and get food for the groups of ants, or colony.

Some parts of the ants' underground homes are for eggs

FACT: In many cases, ants from one colony do not get along with ants from another colony. This is not always true, though. In Melbourne, Australia, ants have joined into one huge supercolony. This colony is so big that it stretches for 100 kilometers (62 miles).

Queen ant and worker ants

and some for larvae (baby ants), which hatch from the eggs. Yet other parts are for storing food, and some are for queen ants. A queen ant does not work like worker ants. Her job is to lay eggs that will become new ants.

 ## Ideas for Your Science Fair

- What kind of food do ants seem to like?
- How far away can ants be and still find their way back to their home?
- What happens to an ant's home after a heavy rainstorm?

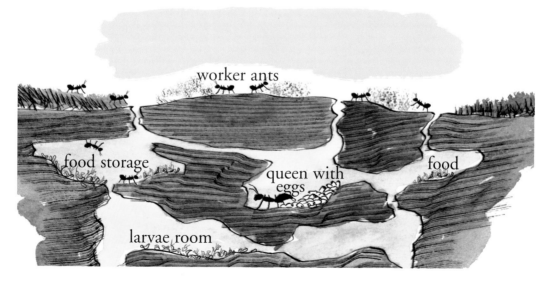

worker ants

food storage

queen with eggs

food

larvae room

Which Tiny Animal Moves Most Quickly?

How quickly can different tiny animals move across a surface? Write down your ideas and your reasons for them.

Now Let's Find Out!

1   Look at each of the tiny animals with your magnifying glass. What body parts do they use to get around? Which do you think could move most quickly across a smooth surface? Why?

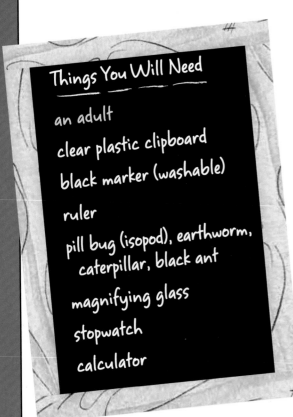

Things You Will Need

an adult

clear plastic clipboard

black marker (washable)

ruler

pill bug (isopod), earthworm, caterpillar, black ant

magnifying glass

stopwatch

calculator

2   Use a washable marker to draw a starting line across the top of your clipboard. **Ask an adult** to hold the plastic clipboard above your head.

3 Place the first animal onto the starting line. Using the stopwatch and the magnifying glass, observe how far each animal travels in 15 seconds. Measure and record that distance in centimeters.

4 Divide the distance traveled by 15 (the seconds it traveled). This is the animal's speed in centimeters per second.

5 Which animals had the quickest speed on the smooth surface? Why do you think this happened? When you are finished, take the animals outside and let them go in a safe area.

Which Tiny Animal Moves Most Quickly?

An Explanation

Tiny animals travel at different speeds depending on the shape and number of body parts that move them along. Animals with short legs and segments, like earthworms, pill bugs, and caterpillars, move slowly along a smooth surface. It helps these animals to have a bumpy surface to grab onto.

FACT: Caterpillars move in a very special way. Scientists and engineers study them to figure out exactly how they move across a surface. "Caterpillar motion" is used in vehicles that have to go over uneven ground.

Bulldozer with caterpillar treads

Ants have six legs that keep their bodies higher off the ground than the other small animals. This helps ants to move more quickly across a smooth surface.

 ## Ideas for Your Science Fair

- Which animal is fastest in climbing up a tilted surface: caterpillar, ant, pill bug, or earthworm?

- Do earthworms travel in the same way over a wet surface as they do over a dry surface?

- Do earthworms travel over a cold surface at the same speed as they do over a warm surface?

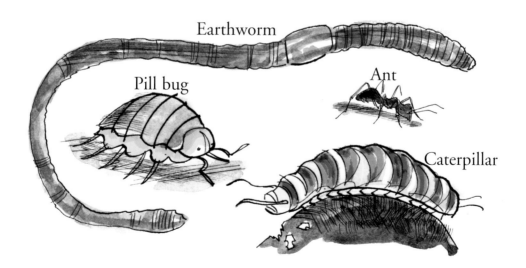

Earthworm

Pill bug

Ant

Caterpillar

Experiment 5
What Body Parts Do All Insects Have?

In what ways are insects alike? Write down your ideas and your reasons for them.

Now Let's Find Out!

1 **Ask an adult** to punch holes in each of the lids, put each insect into its own jar and put on its lid. Observe the insects carefully from all sides with your magnifying glass.

Things You Will Need

an adult

3 different non-stinging or non-biting insects (grasshopper, beetle, black ant, moth)

3 large clear plastic jars with lids

magnifying glass

2 In what ways are the insects the same? How many legs does each one have? How many body sections? Do they all have the same number of eyes?

3 How are the insects different? Look at their colors, shapes, and sizes. Do they all have wings?

22

If so, are the wings in the same place on all the insects?

4 What other insects do you know about? How are they the same and different from the ones in your jar?

5 When you are finished observing your insects, release them into a safe place outdoors.

What Body Parts Do All Insects Have?

An Explanation

All insects are alike in some ways. They all have six legs and three body sections. The three body sections are the head, the thorax (chest), and the abdomen. The legs and wings are attached to the thorax. The abdomen is usually the largest part of the insect.

Many insects have "compound" eyes. This means each

FACT: Scientists have identified over 900 thousand species of insects in the world. There are many more that have still not been discovered. Eighty percent of the animal species in the whole world are insects!

Damselfly

main eye has many tiny eyes within it. Some insects have more than two eyes.

Insects can be very different in many ways. Some, like butterflies, have wings; others do not. Some have stingers (bees and wasps), and others, like mosquitoes, bite. Insects can also live in many different places.

 ## Ideas for Your Science Fair

- What types of insects are there around your area in warm weather?

- What food attracts butterflies to a feeder?

- How long does it take a mealworm to grow from an egg to an adult?

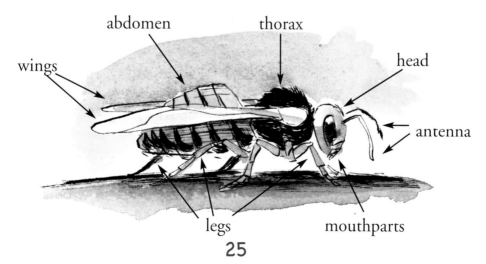

abdomen   thorax

wings   head

antenna

legs   mouthparts

What Animals Live in Different Kinds of Soil?

Do different types of animals live in different types of soil? Write down your ideas and your reasons for them.

Now Let's Find Out!

1 **Ask an adult** to help you find two different kinds of soil (sandy, clay, or humus). Try digging in your backyard, a garden, or vacant lot. Dig down about 18 centimeters (8 inches) so that you have a good chance of finding animals. Put about 2 cups of soil in each bag.

2 Spread out your sheet of white paper. Draw a line down the center of the paper. Put the soil from your two plastic bags on either side of the line.

Things You Will Need

an adult

trowel

ruler

2 plastic bags

2 plastic spoons

large sheet of white paper

magnifying glass

paper and pencil

3 Use the plastic spoons to spread out the soil. Use the magnifying glass and the spoons to find whatever animals you can in the two soils.

4 Are the animals the same in both types of soil? How are they different, if at all? What kinds of animals seem to like which type of soil? Why do you think that?

5 Record your observations about the soil-dwelling animals. Be sure to wash your hands after you clean up the soil. Put the soil and animals back where you found them.

What Animals Live in Different Kinds of Soil?

An Explanation

Many types of animals live underground in soil. Earthworms, grubs, and pill bugs like soil that holds water well, like clay and humus. Ants tend to make their home in sandy soil that they can use to make ant homes. Animals that live in soil are able to burrow and move through spaces between bits of soil.

FACT: The cicada insect lives underground for most of its life. It lives there by sucking sap out of tree roots. One type of cicada only comes out of the ground every 17 years! They stay up just long enough to find a mate, lay hundreds of eggs, and then die.

Cicada out of the ground after 17 years

There are many other types of living things in soil that are too small for you to see without a microscope.

 ## Ideas for Your Science Fair

- What do soil-dwelling animals do when it rains?
- What do soil-dwelling animals eat?
- What happens when you bring soil-dwelling animals to the soil's surface?

clay soil with earthworm
and pill bugs

sandy soil
with ants

Experiment 7
Which Foods Do Goldfish Prefer?

Do goldfish prefer goldfish food from the pet store or fresh lettuce? Write down your ideas and your reasons for them.

Now Let's Find Out!

1   With the help of **an adult**, set up the aquarium according to the directions that come with it. When the water in the aquarium is ready, add the two goldfish.

2   On the first day the goldfish are in the aquarium, read the fish food package to see how much to feed the fish. Weigh out this amount on the kitchen scale. Record the amount in your notebook.

Things You Will Need

an adult

small aquarium

two small common goldfish

kitchen scale

fresh lettuce leaves, such as finely shredded iceberg

flake goldfish food from a pet store

notebook and pen

3 Feed the fish the flake goldfish food. Make sure you do not overfeed them. Observe what the fish do with the food.

4 On the second day, feed the fish the same weight of shredded lettuce as you did the flake goldfish food. What do they do with the food this time?

5 On the third day, put in a combination of the flake food and the lettuce. Do they seem to like one food more than the other?

Which Foods Do Goldfish Prefer?

An Explanation

There are many different kinds of goldfish. Not all goldfish like the same kinds of food, but common goldfish usually prefer flake fish food specially made for them. They may also like to eat lettuce and even shelled peas.

Goldfish keep eating even after they are full, so it is important not to overfeed them.

FACT: Common goldfish can live for many years if they are well cared for. They need to have clean water, the right kind and amount of food, and warm temperatures. A goldfish, in England, called Tish, died in 1999 after living 43 years!

Common goldfish

Ideas for Your Science Fair

- How do goldfish behave when you come near their tank?

- What type of fish food do neon tetras prefer?

- Can goldfish be trained to respond to different colors?

Common goldfish

Redcap goldfish

What Birds Come at Different Times of Year?

Do the same birds visit your neighborhood throughout the year? Write down your ideas and your reasons for them.

Now Let's Find Out!

1 You will be looking for birds at different times of the year, so this project will take a long time. Set aside a place to keep your bird-watching notebook and field guide so that you can always find them.

2 With the help of an adult, find a good place to watch for birds. It might be in your backyard or a nearby field or park. The bird feeder will help to attract the birds. Practice using the binoculars so that you can spot birds quickly.

Things You Will Need

an adult
good place for bird-watching
   (backyard, park, school
   yard, nature center, field)
bird feeder
bird field guide
binoculars
outdoor thermometer
notebook and pen

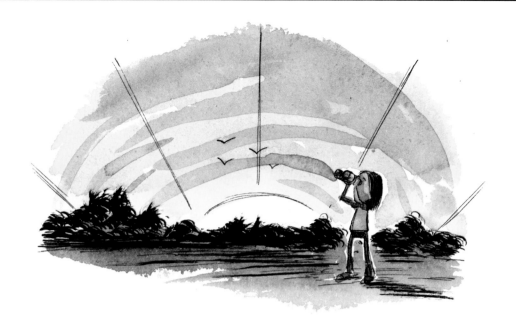

3 Plan on doing your bird-watching once a week. Try to do it at the same time of day. Write down the outdoor temperature in your notebook and the date and time of day. Also write what the weather is like. As you spot a bird, record what it is in your notebook.

4 If possible, keep your record over a year. Look back over your record. Did the same birds show up all year? If not, what different birds showed up in warm temperatures and cold temperatures? Talk to an adult about birds in past years. Does he or she remember seeing the same kinds of birds that you see now?

What Birds Come at Different Times of Year?

An Explanation

You will see different kinds of birds in your neighborhood depending upon where you live and what the season is. Birds come at different times for food. They also come at different times to breed their young.

In areas where the temperatures change a lot during the year, people can see a wide variety of birds. They might see

FACT: Some birds travel amazing distances to their breeding grounds. A bird called the sooty shearwater travels 65,000 kilometers (40,000 miles) from where it breeds to where its feeding grounds are. Scientists have tracked it from New Zealand to California and other western states.

Sooty shearwater

robins in the spring, goldfinches in the summer, and cardinals in the winter. In areas where the temperature stays warm all year long, there may be less bird variety.

 ## Ideas for Your Science Fair

- Do the birds that you see in spring stay all spring, or do they come and go?

- Where do birds in your neighborhood make their nests?

- How do birds in your neighborhood behave when they are startled or frightened?

Blue jay in winter

Robin in spring

What Happens When You Change a Pet's Routine?

What happens when you change how your pet sleeps or eats? Write down your ideas and your reasons for them.

Now Let's Find Out!

1 Talk with **an adult** about what to change in your pet's routine. What will be interesting to observe, but not upset your pet? You could change the feeding time, or the place where the pet's food dish is. You might move your pet's bed or change the furniture around where your pet sleeps.

Things You Will Need

an adult

pet (for example: cat, dog, bird, hamster, etc.)

pet food dish and food

pet bed or other possession (rug, blanket)

2 Once you make the change, observe what your pet does over three days. Does it adapt to the change? How do you know that your pet notices the change?

Does your pet try to put things back the way they were or does it make a new routine?

3 At the end of three days, put things back the way they were and watch your pet. What happens this time?

What Happens When You Change a Pet's Routine?

An Explanation

Your pet has a routine, just like you do. It expects to get its food in the same place and time. It likes to sleep in the same spot (or at least a spot that it chooses).

Some pets can adapt to changes more easily than others. Usually, the more intelligent the pet, the more adaptable it is, but this is not always true.

FACT: The ancient Egyptians were the first to tame cats as pets around 4,000 years ago. The cats killed mice and other pests. Cats became so popular in ancient Egypt that parents even named their children after cats!

Egyptian statue of cat goddess

Some very intelligent pets get very upset when their routines are changed.

 ## Ideas for Your Science Fair

- Which pets seem to like routines more, cats or dogs?

- How do pets respond when they get special food treats?

- How do your pets respond to new food?

Experiment 10
Can You Train Goldfish?

Is it possible to train goldfish to come when you give them a signal? Write down your ideas and your reasons for them.

Now Let's Find Out!

1 With the help of **an adult**, set up the aquarium according to the directions that come with it. When the water in the aquarium is ready, add the two goldfish.

Things You Will Need

an adult

10-gallon aquarium with filter and pump

2 common goldfish

goldfish food, either flake or pellets

strong flashlight

notebook and pen

2 Feed the goldfish from the same side of the tank at the same time of day for three days. (Make sure that you give them the right amount of food.) Observe what the goldfish do when you sprinkle in the food.

3 On the fourth day, turn on the flashlight just before you

42

feed the fish. Turn it off when the fish are finished eating. Over the next three days, again turn on the flashlight just before you feed the fish and off when they are done.

4 On the fourth day, move the flashlight to the other side of the aquarium. Turn it on, but do not feed the fish for a while. Observe what the fish do. Will they come to the other side of the aquarium just for the light signal? Do they need to be fed at the same time to get them to come to that side? Experiment with the light in different places and see how long the fish will come and stay if they do not get fed right afterward.

Can You Train Goldfish?
An Explanation

Goldfish are sensitive to light. When feeding time is combined with a bright light, the goldfish begin to link the light with food. Once they have made the link, they will keep coming to the light even if there is no food, at least for a while.

Over time, the goldfish will stop coming to the light if they do not get rewarded with food.

FACT: Using food as a reward, goldfish have been trained to do some amazing things. One fish, "Albert Einstein," is able to push a tiny soccer ball into a net. He can also catch rings with his head and go through a kind of obstacle course.

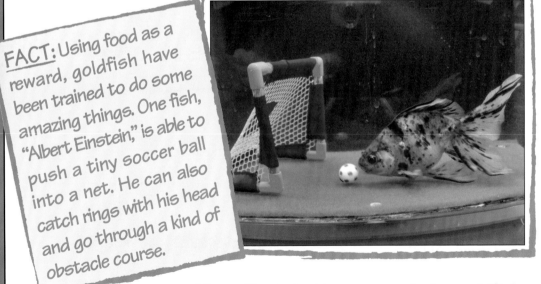

Albert Einstein, the soccer-playing goldfish

Ideas for Your Science Fair

- How can you train your goldfish to do tricks?
- Can goldfish be trained to respond to sounds?
- Will guppies respond to light?

Words To Know

adapted—To be suited to a habitat.

aquarium—A water tank that holds fish and other living things.

binoculars—Tools you can use to see things that are far away.

field guide—A book you can use to identify animals, like birds.

habitat—A place where an organism lives.

humus—Material in soil that came from once living things.

insect—A small animal with six legs and three body sections.

isopod—An animal with a flattened body and seven pairs of legs.

mate—How animals produce their young.

microscope—A tool to help see very tiny things.

organism—A living thing.

organs—Parts of living things that do special jobs.

prostomium—The fleshy area above an earthworm's mouth.

sensitive—To react easily to something, like light or sound.

species—A grouping of organisms.

Learn More

Books

Bochinski, Julianne Blair. *The Complete Workbook for Science Fair Projects.* Hoboken, N.J.: Wiley, 2005.

Hickman, Pamela. *Animals in Motion: How Animals Swim, Jump, Slither and Glide.* Toronto: Kids Can Press, Ltd., 2000.

O'Neill, Amanda. *Insects and Bugs.* New York: Kingfisher, 2002.

Kittinger, Jo S. *Smithsonian Kids' Field Guides: Birds of North America East.* New York: DK Publishing, 2001.

Internet Addresses

National Geographic Kids. "Animals."
http://kids.nationalgeographic.com/

National Wildlife Federation. "Kids and Families."
http://www.nwf.org/kids/

Smithsonian Institution. "AnimalCams."
http://nationalzoo.si.edu/Animals/WebCams/

Index